To a Fault

To a Fault

Nick Laird

W. W. Norton & Company   New York   London

First published in 2005 by Faber and Faber Limited

Copyright © 2005 by Nick Laird
First American Edition 2006

For information about permission to reproduce selections from this book, write to
Permissions, W. W. Norton & Company, Inc., 500 Fifth Avenue, New York, NY 10110

Manufacturing by The Courier Companies, Inc.
Book design by Anna Oler
Production manager: Amanda Morrison

Library of Congress Cataloging-in-Publication Data

Laird, Nick, 1975–
   To a fault / Nick Laird.—1st American ed.
      p. cm.
   ISBN-13: 978-0-393-06186-4
   ISBN-10: 0-393-06186-8
   I. Title.
   PR6112.A35T6 2006
   823'.92—dc22

                                    2005038012

W. W. Norton & Company, Inc.
500 Fifth Avenue, New York, N.Y. 10110
www.wwnorton.com

W. W. Norton & Company Ltd.
Castle House, 75/76 Wells Street, London W1T 3QT

1 2 3 4 5 6 7 8 9 0

for Lady Z

Acknowledgements

I gratefully acknowledge the editors of the publications where the following poems have appeared: *Colorado Review* ('An Evening Forecast for the Region', 'The Riddles of the Ardcumber Book'); *New Writing 11* (Picador; 'Firmhand the Queried', 'The Last Saturday in Ulster'); *Poetry Review* ('Disclaimer', 'Done', 'The Bearhug'); *London Review of Books* ('Imperial', 'The Layered', 'The Gritter'); *Times Literary Supplement* ('A Portrait of the Artist as a Joke', 'Cuttings', 'The Eventual', 'Remaindermen', 'Poetry'); *The Guardian* ('The Last Saturday in Ulster', 'Pedigree'); *Time Out* ('To the Wife'); *The Times* ('The Fault').

I thank the Society of Authors for an Eric Gregory Award.

Many thanks also to Jorie Graham for her encouragement and advice.

Contents

To a Fault

Cuttings

Methodical dust shades the combs and pomade
while the wielded goodwill of the sunlight picks out
a patch of paisley wallpaper to expand leisurely on it.

The cape comes off with a matador's flourish
and the scalp's washed to get rid of the chaff.
This is the closeness casual once in the trenches

and is deft as remembering when not to mention
the troubles or women or prison.
They talk of the parking or calving or missing.

A beige lino, a red barber's chair, one ceramic brown sink
and a scenic wall-calendar of the glories of Ulster
sponsored by JB Crane Hire or some crowd flogging animal feed.

About, say, every second month or so
he will stroll and cross the widest street in Ireland
and step beneath the bandaged pole.

Eelmen, gunmen, the long dead, the police.
And my angry and beautiful father:
tilted, expectant and open as in a deckchair

outside on the drive, persuaded to wait
for a meteor shower, but with his eyes budded shut,
his head full of lather and unusual thoughts.

The Given

At first they took the gift of smell. Oh well,
we never used it much though once or twice
it let us know we hadn't lit the gas.
We bit our tongues then said *Yes, help yourself.*
It is accepted we're losing our senses.

Last year they came, unpeeled each ear. Oh dear,
we couldn't hear the cars come near and once
or twice we got ourselves in accidents.
At night we fingertip each other's breath to check.
We held our tongues then said, *Here, take the rest.*

On Tuesday laws were passed to snatch our taste.
It's no great waste. Our appetites and cigarettes
had put those tastebuds to the test so as for us
we swallowed tongues then shrugged to say *Go right ahead.*
As long as they stay, we sit on our hands.

Days diminish. Today they confiscated touch.
We can guess how hot the water is,
and in darkness estimate the distance to the bed.
To accept these losses, we cover our faces,
then scratch *Be our guest* with a fork on the table.

And then tonight they came for sight. We knew they might.
A minute back they turned into our street.
The door we've blocked with books now shakes.
We play them tapes we had prepared
then hiss and mouth our tongueless chorus.

But of course they cannot see of course.

Poetry

It's a bit like looking through the big window
on the top deck of the number 47.

I'm watching you, and her, and all of them,
but through my own reflection.

Or opening my eyes when everyone's praying.
The wave machine of my father's breathing,

my mother's limestone-fingered steeple,
my sister's tiny fidgets, and me, moon-eyed, unforgetting.

And then the oak doors flapping slowly open to let us out,
like some great injured bird trying to take flight.

The Length of a Wave

At the mythic coast, by the kitchen stove,
my father warms his back and talks of floods,
riptides, the boy drowned in Bundoran.

My mother thinks his moods dependent on the moon,
and this, I think, is a non-trivial thing.
He broke the light switch twice by punching it.

Outside, his voice would echo off John Faulkner's hill
and I could judge the playground's width, the distance
of the storm, by knowing how sound travels.

Now I wait for your letter and get to work late.

This scale I'm calibrating spans from the bomb
to the corpses in the mortuary awaiting recognition.
In between I've notched in other soundings:

the barley banger four fields over,
the gonging of the garage door by tennis balls
then ordinary speech, and under that

an adult seagull's flight, at six or seven feet,
the whispering of next door's cistern,
the tidal breathing of your sleeping,

and a struck match's dry whistle.

Although an ear, I've heard, for resonant frequencies
means one should speak of the droning Chinook,
the domestic slap of the rifle's crack,

systolic summer Lambeg nights, a sea in earshot
of the fields where mushrooms scatter, moon-pale,
amazed, like faces upturned to a tidal wave,

because across those miles of hills and dark
the squares of light are quartered flags
hung out to mark the embassies of Home,

where to stay intact's to show your only handsome side —

your back, and where he'd shout from his armchair,
Put your hand to the door. Are you coming in or out?
I'm still not sure. The last flight

would get me back to Donegal by dawn,
to where he nightly watched the sun go down.
I could park and watch light complicate the water,

or wade out through the stinging cold saltwater,
which among its many noted uses
is reputed to be good for cleaning silver,

cutlery, or jewellery, and disinfecting wounds.

The Fault

You woke me and I stood and looked,
astounded, put my foot in it,

withdrew then what I could of it,
'cause come the revolution

of the earth,
the rule is crockery's the first

against the wall,
the reverse of which

I'm rapt with as we each
dissemble sleep, but wait,

and listen to the darkness fidget:
it sucks in its gut, lights up,

and swears under its breath
as it struts through the flat,

unzipping the lino, not stopping
until it's laid down in the slit,

and dared us to watch it,
to hopscotch across its display

of the meanings of cleave,
and accept this is what saves us

from sweeping the kitchen,
and stops us from sleeping.

Remaindermen

Because what I liked about them best
was their ability to thole,
that weathered silence and reluctance,
fornenst the whole damn lot.

They've lived alone for years of course,
and watched their cemeteries filling up
like car parks on a Saturday,
their young grow fat for export.

There are others who know what it is
to lose, to hold ideas of north
so singularly brutal that the world
might be ice-bound for good.

Someone has almost transcribed
the last fifty years of our speech,
and has not once had the chance
to employ the word *sorry*

or press the shift to make the mark
that indicates the putting of a question.
The arch was put up wrong this Spring
outside my father's office.

When you enter it states
Safe Home Brethren,
and upon leaving the place
Welcome Here.

The Signpost

Knee-capped on the second Tuesday of the month
by two of the stringy cunts
he'd last bought a round for at Christmas

put paid to the plans for ascending Everest,
and playing for Rangers, even in goal
(though it left open Glentoran, as his father'd suggested).

*

The pistol jammed and they kicked him over.
They could break his legs, they offered,
but he waited, and another gun was brought,

and the barrel held against his calf
(friends, see, so they spared his knees),
and the trigger pulled and the bullet shot.

*

Opening fire: slitting the skin of the side of the flame.
He'd held a bomb the same weight as he'd been when born.
Pan back. Agree with that, the thought he had until he blacked,

what with one arm splayed under, and the other
swung over the blade of his shoulder,
he must, from above, make sense as a signpost.

*

From the Royal's window he got a clear view.
An air vent on a roof lent a heat haze to Belfast,
and two cranes swung their arms low over the city,

as if giving a blessing. Incredible to stay upright
with all that gathered weight. He spied his father's house,
but all the lights, strange that, were out.

Imperial

'And should I not pity Nineveh, that great city, in which there
are more than a hundred and twenty thousand persons who do not
know their right hand from their left, and also much cattle?'

—*Jonah 4:11*

1

In *A Popular Account of Discoveries at Nineveh* (1854)
Austin Henry Layard, the popular archaeologist and author,
is again among the ruins by the dying of October,

scattering some Arabs from a hostile tribe among the rest
to keep acquainted with what's said in tents behind his back
and attentive to the threat of pilfered relics.

When he isn't concluding *a few summary punishments*
to check the drawing of sabres and priming of matchlocks
or how the male Musselman is naturally this or commonly that,

he will ease pieces out from the flesh of the earth
as a midwife might, to weigh and catalogue and wrap
the objects for their journey, by way of Busrah and Baghdad,

buffalo-carts of the pashaw and willow-rafts on the Tigris,
to the pale hands in the cool basement of the British Museum.

2

Layard watches oxen, harnessed on slopes built into the bank,
counterweighting a bucket, the entire skin of a bullock,

which sinks down into the stream. Come late afternoon,
the cattle lay down in each other's shadows.

Excavating the southern entrance to the north-west palace,
a limestone winged lion is exhumed, and inlaid above the wings:

A human figure, and a monster with the head of a lion,
the body of a man, and the feet of a bird, raising a sword.

Assyria dealt in fear. The Sargonids were politic and vicious.
But a voice from the south, a preacher repeating his God,

Yet forty days, and Nineveh shall be o'erthrown.

Stripped of sackcloth, the saved resume their businesses.
The buying and selling of incense, terebinth, currency, time.
Outside the city, Jonah lies down beside his dying gourd.

3

The cattle graze behind fences of cedar or, herded,
are ambling down to the river to drink
in the time between milking and darkness.

They follow, obedient,
uninterested, swinging the sacks
of themselves down the dust tracks towards dusk.

Can they remember?
They catalogue hurt.

At the enclosure of night they lift gazes to prophets,
to a white man on horseback, to Ninivite warriors,
to the slip of a cowherd who keeps them,
to Jonah, the moon, whoever is there,

pool-eyed and aware
how close they come.

4

Gertrude Bell is spending a pleasant afternoon riding over
the Mesopotamian desert. The Great War has ended.
She trails a walking stick behind her in the sand to mark a boundary
as Arab boys build cairns on it to set frontiers for these new countries.

The cattle wear down their paths into roads
and the rivers move under the borders.

The kingdom of here. Relics and oilfields.
Satellites mistaken for portents. The engine of man is desire.
We are again among these ruins and the dying.

*A human figure, and a monster with the head of a lion,
the body of a man, and the feet of a bird, raising a sword.*

A line in the sand begins to unwind in the machinery of wind
which starts up and ticks over as the flies come to grief
and the cattle lie down in each other's shelter.

The Gritter

It could almost be harvesting ice,
what with that chaff, this sluice of lost fillings,
pellets from airguns, breadcrumbs and grape pips,
these infinite clippings of night.
They scatter. They generate weather.
And flesh the road from bone to wound. Open.

The gritter makes unhurried circular journeys
like the drunk in a child's anorak
who nightly would slope his resolute ghost
out through the pub and then once into dawn,
found dead, face down, detaining the herd
on their way to be milked at some farm.

They stand patiently round him like mourners
then veer off in groups. Their breath clears like smoke.
This might be the end of an all-night party:
potholes like punchbowls, a grass-tinselled verge,
thawed drops of birdsong prodding the straggler
to tell him it's time to get up and go home,

but he won't sleep this off, won't wake
surprised and wander back to town alone
through swift new snow that's falling now
too heavily to leave the myth
of how those flakes are each distinct,
like fingerprints, like skin, intact.

The Mouth of the Sea

The helicopter landed and fastened itself to the beach.
It shuddered and spun great billowed sheets
of sand out towards the waves.

Turk and I waded in from the water,
quick and curious, and stood wrapped
in towels to watch the chain of rowing boats

round the headland and cross the horizon.
The clouds were wearing a pendant,
one that none would dare call *sun*

when the boats are packed with upright men
staring through reflections for such a thing,
but with a face grown swollen, pale as moon,

unkempt, as after sleep, wreathed in kelp and dulse.
The pilot said a boy from Kesh got lost last night
when a trawler couped after coming round Kildoney Point.

A storm broke as they crossed the bar,
where the sea meets the mouth of the river,
or the river meets the mouth of the sea.

Cycling through Snow and Fields
on New Year's Eve

this time last year I queued outside
with charlie, pills, two wraps of speed
my pupils bloomed with atmosphere
I'd smoked at least an ounce of weed

my oldest friend who's come out queer
had got inside an hour before
but reappeared to nick some blow
then shimmied back into the bar

I'm cycling through the folded snow
down unsung lanes in mid-Tyrone
and score a line that could be read
same-old same-old you know so-so

I could lay down my snowbound head —
the field is gone and is instead
a sheet that covers up the dead —
but freewheel home and slip inside

The Rope Bridge

You cross the rope bridge as you talk,
bypass whistling gaps, keep in step with solid wood,
the hand-rail's grammar, and make it straight over.

No bother. No looking down, no biting your tongue
'til I start and stammer, I pause in the centre,
gape seawards, let fly with these or likewise airy notions,

armsweeps, adjectives, the usual pledges,
obsess on the seawinds, the flightpaths of seabirds,
await balance (these oceans, these edges), but instead

find the head at a loss, at last, for words it can trust.

*

Help me keep a hold of this.
Huddle down and listen with
the man who asks forgiveness,

the one whose swollen tongue has grown
to fill, not fit, his frown, and utters lovesongs,
curses, on its own. Let him begin again.

Let him go back and mind his language.
Listen. He picks on scarecrows, skyscrapers,
scapegoats, smallish lexical mercies.

The Bearhug

It's not as if I'm intending on spending the rest of my life
    doing this:
besuited, rebooted, filing to work, this poem a fishbone in
    my briefcase.
The scaffolding clinging St Paul's is less urban ivy than
    skin, peeling off.

A singular sprinkler shaking his head spits at the newsprint
    of birdshit.
It's going unread: Gooseberry Poptarts, stale wheaten
    bread, Nutella and toothpaste.
An open-armed crane turns to embrace the aeroplanes
    passing above.

I hadn't the foggiest notion. Imagine: me, munching
    cardboard and rubbish,
but that's just what they meant when they said, *Come in,*
    you're dead-beat,
take the weight off your paws, you're a big weary grizzly
    with a hook through his mouth,

here, have some of this love.

Aubade

Go home. I haven't slept alone
in weeks and need to reach across
the sheets to find not warmth but loss.

The lack of which now sees me fat
and not content — by that I mean
I couldn't manage either tough or kind.

Not fit to speak to man or beast,
I wouldn't suffer you to see
the sight of me drawn inside-out,

which means the thing is being there.
Not here. If you knew enough you'd
know removed is how you're loved.

Get up. Take yourself into the night.
Walk streets that lie against and cross
themselves to pray for shade, then light.

Disclaimer

It's not the flyer on the windscreen or cross-examination
and neither is it hatemail to the dead.
It's not a flight card or the black box's recordings.

It's not a self-help guide on weight loss or grief
or something you'd tell your friend's wife,
and it's never enough for the mortgage.

It's not a space on the floor to lie down on.
Or a bloodstain on the front of a shirt.
Not memorable speech and not legalese.

Not the sepia evening you almost were hitched
to the idea of your high-school sweetheart, and nor is it
the tremulous blow job you got in the Eurostar toilet

from the psychology student who sat opposite.
Though there are certain noises, the clattering of horses,
or the trees outside just now, which have been heard forever,

and I wonder what they meant back when —
like this wind I mean,
this off-key persistent whistling.

Whatever it is, it's not only a judgement or pleading.
Not just a smallholding. Not just moving parts.
And it's not all the same.

It is joined-up writing.
It's not lifting the pen from this page.

Corridorsong

Started out a xylem cell in
a snowdrop's bell-pull stem,

and got promoted fast
to the see-through shaft

of a ball-point pen,
though after that: pure graft —

fed up with the cuffs
of a well-dressed corpse,

I was granted a paragraph,
translated to Dutch,

and then made the dry bed
of a river in Kansas,

before they offered me this
windowless passage

where I wait until winter
when I will retire

to a firebreak sunk
like the wake of a harvester

and set to prevent, so I'm told,
the relentless spread of the word

The Downpour

Two cubes in a polished highball glass,
a double shot of chilled and Polish vodka,
a citrus twist and fresh tomato juice
to bring it to the brim,
three spins of Lea & Perrins,
a dab of sharp Tabasco . . .

Four of us darting as if the floor and bar surface
are hot as a colliery furnace,
and to which in all fairness
this place bears a resemblance
after ten hours at a time pulling pints,
fishing bottles of beer from buckets of ice.

The punters outside are half-cut and shirty.
I've been doing all doubles at work.
What looked like a fridge in a river was not
but an ambulance reeled to the gathered nearspace
of the girl who got smashed, with a glass, in the face.
The temperature here's been skirting round thirty.

On scuffed broken tarmac blood serum
is several shades darker than you ever remember.
The weather comes loose like a bandage.
The downpour is fingers tapping the bar.
The last man to leave is encouraged
to stand and slowly led out like a victim.

Firmhand the Queried

1

I remember poncing a fag off some guy at the bar,
then downing the dregs of my last pint of stout,
spotting the wink of the head of the state,
then pinkie rings denting my flesh epaulettes,

waking alone on the floor of the gents
with the unshakeable sense that the room was afloat,
bracing myself with the sink and hand-dryer,
then eying the blur swimming up through the mirror,

which seemed vaguely familiar, and I remember
being dimly aware I was late for somewhere.

2

A slow and dry-mouthed stretch of night:
the heating's sad machinery sleeptalks
its poem through the firedoors' artillery,
paper cuts, Windsor knots, artificial light,

an Anglepoise so annoyed the cords in its neck
tilt at full stretch as it poses and tuts like
a gull on the deck, that, and the daily weight
of being unable to swim, idling the plank

of the corridor, and diving beneath the desk
when someone tried to give me work.

3

But, flexing the strut of my glossy umbrella,
I scarcely remember snapping the throat
of a cormorant caught in the dragnet, though their
similar colour — shrink-wrapped street — and angular

shape — knocked-over ink — brought it back
to the poems shipwrecked on Manila
that fight over deadlines, tiepins, doubloons,
and a map on a beermat that might just disclose

a reef offroute to planes and ships, where the natives refuse
to keep off the grass and wear garlands of pea-green paperclips.

4

I was whistling the secret last note of its anthem
as my pen bloomed through Armani and onto my shirt.
I stagewhispered help before faking a swoon,
and left the CCTV a last grainy shot of a door, swinging shut.

I leapt astern in a harbourtown famed for its spice
and honey-thick silks, and there I was showing the locals
that to stand on a chair completely changes your view
when I fell off and came to in this bar. I don't know you

but if you have questions, drink late at the establishment
down by the river. You will find it both new and strangely familiar.

The Eventual

Your hands surprising at the station,
shinycold and taut as plumskin, late.

It could have been All Hallows' Eve:
me kidding, ripping open Cox's pippins,

you sombre, the counter in the kitchen,
water in the basin dammed with apples.

*

Like a bag of unlabelled bulbs,
the fireworks wanted the precise

release of soluble tablets
to flash their toothless yawn, and shut,

anemone-abruptly, on such a glossy dark
the laundered hail was frictionless and filmic.

*

If a long retreat was both giving in to gravity
and growing up, if Jumping Jack Flash

and the Catherine Wheel signed themselves
to the eventual, then things called true

were caught and missed by you,
trepanned windfalls, ghost trains home.

A Portrait of the Artist as a Joke

And yet slaughter may also be a plural of laughter . . .
—*Javier Rodrigues Rodrigues (translated by Joseph Coleman)*

I've heard it told by someone else like this:
an Englishman, an Irishman, a Scot,
all down the Union, slaughtered, lairy, and

the rest's a slow ascending followed by a drop.
I smoked and skimmed the smeary glass,

my diving watch, the Guinness sign behind
the gin, and saw three grinning faces mouth:
Your man walks into a bar, an iron bar . . . ouch.

*

Midway there will be wishes, wives, islands
quietly deserted, jungle tribes, firing squads,
last requests and genies bottled in the jacks.

The finish sees the jars tide-marked, abandoned
to prehensile smoke, the ripped-out wiring

of air that hangs like gags told donkeys back
which weren't too great the first time round.
So please, no laughter, and please, no applause.

*

Each time a round unleashes glass into shocking,
solid rain, and the pub airpockets, shudders, roots,
there's an ovation into the bogs. Some fat fuck's

thumped in the gut and bundled away in a Corsa.
The moon, an unexpected exit wound, rises

to flood the carpark. Someone else can
expand about jokes and the unconscious,
and someone else can refer to the luck of the Irish.

*

In the rough to the left of the fairway
the same man who walked into the bar
lies doubled up with laughter.

The clownery of his ungentle, eggshelled face
is about to break into a grin,

the one last seen in sky-blue morning dress
astride his Samsung wide-screen.
Chances are someone else won't be starting with him.

*

The daymoon eases downwards like a drop
of condensation, and golf caps advertising
legendary local names are doffed, then someone coughs,

clicks off the dawning chorus of his watch.
The secret of good comedy.

The way the horizon nearly stops
the moon's outstretched communion tongue,
like a punchline momentarily forgotten.

The Layered

doubt

Empty Laird was called that 'cause
his Christian name was Matthew
and his middle one was Thomas.

Towards the end he commented
that by his-self he'd made a sixth
of the disciples, and forgone a life

on the quest for the rest.
And a good book.
Or a decent cause.

fear

Laird Jnr was a tyke, a terrier.

A nit-picker who grew to a hair-splitter,
he was not so much scared of his shadow,
as of its absence. He knew he was see-thru.

It was a very modern kind of terror.

lust

the one   who went on to become   Mrs Laird
the wife   walked into my life
one night   I'd had six or seven pints

and it was either that or fight

she was just the type   I like
chest spilling out of itself   slender-hipped
with a Nubian face closed to the public
waist   my exact hand-span

poised and filmic   she was drinking my usual
unthinkable and very
very do-able   I am not a good man
into my grave into my grave into my grave she was laid

Animals

The strangest thing? My tongue.
It thickened like an icicle inside my mouth,
and made me yawp in agony,

that dialect us lot converse in fluently.
They brandished fists, the muzzle of a gun,
a children's torch, and held me down.

I had a day to disappear and stay that way for good.
I sloped at dusk into the hills behind the town:
ate grass, drank piss, kipped in a cow-ditch,

but a dawn arrived where I woke,
mid-lope, scuttling over lucky heather,
bone-cold and aware of the space

between the lifted and the settling paw,
between that which holds and that which goes,
and how it is diminished into choice.

Right then I chose to rejoin — by which I mean
to answer, sharply, and I reappeared that afternoon
three years ago to dull the town like rain.

I called on every man and gave each man his due.
Now I will not speak when spoken to
or sleep a whole night through.

I am Wolfshead.
The Open-Jaw, the Called-Upon,
the Man They Made, and well, of War.

Scarewolf

The modern word scarecrow is the only survivor of a group of fear-based older terms . . .

—*Jeffrey Kacirk, The Calendar of Forgotten English, 2002*

The final one was not, as is often thought,
run to ground and caught on Mullan's Bog,
following a month-long hunt from Gortin Glen
to Ardboe Cross and out past hard Strabane:

a malevolent beast, four fat men wide,
stallion-tall and sporting a shimmery hide
constructed from double-stitched buckskin,
tenderised silver and luck, incisors pretending

to tusks, stropped under eyes sunken as buckets,
pupils thrashing like salmon trapped in them,
and which saw each constellation slip and drift
until the sky was emptied out entirely to dark.

Instead, the one my great-to-the-power-of-eight
grandmother kept in the outhouse to feed on scraps
leftover from dinner, and keep down rats,
and which outlived the scaredeer and the scaregoose,

the scarefly and scaresinner. With marbles mislaid
in charred grass, it watched and seldom barked.
Less wolf than ghost of dog, what happened was
it coughed, perhaps, and then was done with itching.

The Riddles of the Ardcumber Book

I am sure you're aware of the provenance:
the hearth-tales of the rising and subsequent capture,
the escape to *the dark-mouthed cave* in the Glens

and the mound of loose dirt at the back,
the oak chest, and hidden in it, the linen manuscript
that has underwritten the last twenty years of my life.

The university asked me to translate the text:
it was worthy, discursive, a meditation on sin,
the common Assumptions of various saints.

But it was here in the margins that I found my passion:
twenty-five riddles in a rustic Latin.
Nearly every other scholar overlooked them.

The rest misread them.

But these are the things that came to mean love.

(*the fish is a quiet guest*)

Some claimed them for Tatwine the Mercian
who succeeded Behrthwald as Archbishop,
but if you look closely the styles are entirely different

(I cite Tatwine's fondness for double acrostics).

And neither are these Aldhelm's of Malmesbury
who bequeathed one hundred riddles in perfect hexameters.
Mine came later and from here, over the water,

so you can rule out Eusebius
as the author of these owes nothing to Symphosius,
and any resemblance to others — such as Boniface, say —

perhaps in a single phrase or a singing line —
must be put down to coincidence:
each shield will speak of its wounds.

I think he thought he'd invented the form.

(*the quill is the joy of the sparrow*)

I imagine him as a cowherd bedded in heather,
watching the shifting cross-hatching of shade
in the valley, the day leaving already.

It is apparent he was educated, even a chieftain
fled from the wars of the Ulster Cycle,
maybe from Macha herself, and waiting out time

far from the burning and bloodshed.

I read all this from the questions he sets.
I know him to be quick to flare, but generous, sometimes kind.
The main text is not his. The riddles come nearly a hundred years
    after.

They prevent me from falling. I am not explaining myself.
Like myth, the riddle springs from the need to vest life
in the garb of the coldly fabulous.

He took me aside to show me the world.

(*the fish carries with him his house*)

Mead, a wine cup or chalice, a badger, these are the answers I offer,
a rake, a barnacle goose, a loom, a plough, a sword or a dagger,
a letter-beam cut from the stump of a jetty, a fire,

dough, a stook of barleycorn, a gale, an anchor,
a butterfly-cocoon, winter (or the Word of God), a porcupine,
a bookmoth, a Cross or a sword-rack, cloud and wind, an ox

led into the barn by a dying man, mustard, gold, an onion,
and though Williams considers the final solution
is God, I make a persuasive case

that the answer itself is actually 'riddle'.

Nothing, however, could seem unwiser
than strenuous dogmatising over opinions
which may be abandoned by even their champion.

The seeking, you see, I consider analogous.

(*the snow is a featherless bird*)

Pedigree

There are many of us.

My aunt,
the youngest sister,
is a reformed shoplifter.

An uncle breeds champion bantams.

Another, a pig-farmer,
has a racket smuggling cattle
back and forth and back across
the imaginary border.

Me, I've forty-seven cousins.

A scuffle over rustling sheep
became a stabbing in a bar outside Armagh,
and a murderer swings
from a branch high up in our family tree.

Which isn't a willow.

Instead,
an enormous unruly blackthorn hedge,

inside of which a corpse is tangled,
and sags from branch to branch,
like a dewy web:

a farmer jumped on the road, and strangled,
his pockets emptied

of the stock proceeds from the county fair
by two local Roman Catholic farmhands.

Riots in Donegal town when they were cleared.
And riots again when they were convicted.

I may be out on a limb.

One grandfather, the short-horn cattle dealer,
went bankrupt, calmly smoked his pipe,
and died at forty of lung cancer.

Martha, my grandmother, remade Heathhill a dairy farm
and when the rent man came
my mother'd hide behind the sofa with her brothers.

My father spent his boyhood fishing with a hook and
        tinfoil chocolate wrapper.

He coveted a Davy Crockett hat
and shined the medals of his legendary uncles
who'd all died at the Somme,
the Dragoon Guards of Inniskilling.

He left school without sitting his papers
and my mother dropped out to marry him.

Each evening after work and dinner,
she'd do her OU course,
and heave the brown suitcase of books

from out beneath the rickety, mythical bunks
I shared for ten years with my sister.

There is such a shelter in each other.

And you, you pad from the bathroom to Gershwin,
gentled with freckles and moisturized curves,
still dripping, made new, singing your footprints

as they singe the wood floor,
perfect in grammar and posture.

But before you passed me the phone
you were talking, and I couldn't help but note your tone,
as if you couldn't hear them right,
as if they were maybe calling
not from just across the water
but Timbuktu, or from the moon . . .

At least you can hear me, my darling,
I'm speaking so softly and clearly,
and this is a charge not a pleading.

Oświęcim

Someone has disturbed a hive.
What swell and gut the air and have
a million different particles, are bees,

which we mistake for wind and seeds,
at first, but stride out of the jittered storm
thrilled and breathlessly unharmed.

So somewhere honey might be moving,
lazily, its amber tongue,
among leaf litter, acned bark,

bugs glossy-backed and clockwork
which it tastes and then displays
as proofs of end-stopped histories.

Not hard to conjugate the faces,
shorn and watchful in the hallways,
to anger or lovemaking, freckles,

stutters, drunkenness, book-learning,
to couples sleeping back to back, arriving
laden at a country station in the bleach of dawn.

Help me open up these cases
and place in them some spectacles,
a steel prosthetic foot, a fist of auburn hair,

an empty tin of Dutch shoe polish
and a chipped enamel patterned jug,
a yellow appleblossom-patterned jug,

and set each in a locker at the terminals
of all the major capitals, alongside stolen goods,
and photographs in envelopes, and bombs.

Done

We've come to bag the evidence.
This might be the scene of a murder.
Dustsheets and silence and blame.

The flat empties its stomach into the hall.
We have given back letters and eaten our words.
You wrote off the Volvo. I gave you verrucas.

And like the window of a jeweller's after closing
the shelves in the study offer up nothing.
I slowly take the steps down one by one,

and for the first time maybe,
notice the chaos, the smouldering traffic,
the litter, bystanders, what have you

To The Wife

After this iceblink and sudden death of the mammals —
that wolfhound our youngest will poison with gravy on sponges,
the calf whose back leg you fatally shatter, driving home fast,
too sad, from the clinic — and after neither of us have a mother
or father and we've washed up our minuscule five o'clock dinners,

having pottered around the stores all afternoon, mumbling,
buttonholing assistants to complain about prices or rain,
and change over our eyewear to examine the papers
with that contemptuous squint we'll both have adopted,
and decide how we've read all the books that we will,
and that even those in the end offered hassle and pain,

do you think we could find a way back to an evening
when holding each other will not be about balance
and all of the tunes are inside us and wordless?

Everybody Wears Socks

The islands are having their Lazarus moment,
though it is casual, this, and gradual,
with its usual rustle of hedgerow and duvet,

the seepage of dawn into sky
(no slamming of doors, no burglar alarms),
this will be a natural coming around:

a power cut, say, and the rundown
of batteries occurs on the very same night,
so watches and clocks don't last through the small hours

and everyone wakes up at once (just so)
and because of concluding exhaustion:
no draughts, no plumbing, no knees in the spine

but all of us all of us stumbling
or sloping through lamp-shaded hallways
and into the glare of our showers —

goose-bumped, dried off,
hoking for socks in our cupboards
or drawers, for singles that match,

or come close enough in the pale bedroom light:
tennis and hiking, woollen and cotton,
ribbed, acrylic, patterned and heeled,

flesh-coloured or knitted or tubed,
and then yanking wide curtains of flowers or stripes,
clanking at shutters, retuning outside back in through the blinds,

before slipping on shoes or tying the laces.
We bandage ourselves every morning
and step carefully out as if onto ice.

A blackbird is watching and seems suddenly serious.

On Beauty

No, we could not itemise the list
of sins they can't forgive us.
The beautiful don't lack the wound.
It is always beginning to snow.

Of sins they can't forgive us
speech is beautifully useless.
It is always beginning to snow.
The beautiful know this.

Speech is beautifully useless.
They *are* the damned.
The beautiful know this.
They stand around unnatural as statuary.

They are the damned
and so their sadness is perfect,
delicate as an egg placed in your palm.
Hard, it is decorated with their face

and so their sadness is perfect.
The beautiful don't lack the wound.
Hard, it is decorated with their face.
No, we could not itemise the list.

The Trunk in the Storeroom

I am sitting down to write to you from habit.
I have nothing important to communicate.

Mrs Buchanan's melodeon is of mahogany
and the keys were swollen with the damp weather.
They were so stiff it was almost impossible to play them.
It arrived here from Spirit Lake the day before yesterday.
I am learning Fishers Hornpipe and the Willow Song.

The climate is capricious in the south and east as in the west
and this season much more so.

In Texas to secure crops, early planting becomes necessary.
This exposes the plant to the effect of capricious change of
    temperature.
For this reason Ohio and even Southern Illinois, they say,
are not as certain for fruit as it will be here
where the vegetation has a longer and more even sleep.

I left the jewellery and most of the watches in the Trunk in the
    storeroom.
There was no sale for them. I ceased to value them. I was too
    careless.
For a time the boys slept in the room but this was troublesome and
    was dropt.
The consequence was that some villain took charge of all the good
    articles
including the package of broken Bank Bills that was in the Tin
    box.

HD is suspected and watched closely by several.

On the evening of the first a dry snow commenced its falling
and continued through the night.

We look upon it as providential.

No letters have arrived since I wrote to you last.
I hope you may soon find time to write.

The Last Saturday in Ulster

Behind her radiator
the leather purse is caring
for the old denominations:
liverspots of giant pennies,
fifty pences thick as lenses.

A Pentecostal home outside Armagh:
antimacassars, oxygen masks,
Martha glancing towards the screen
as if checking delay and departure.

An Orange march in Antrim
will see me late arriving:
and standing out at Aldergrove
an English girl might well believe
that time is how you spend your love.

Undriven cattle graze the long acre.
Pheasants fidget and flit between townlands.
The coins were warm as new eggs
in the nest of her priestly-cool hands.

Scenes from the Nativity

With six days to Christmas,
as I fingertip pictures
on your back's narrow canvas
(La Gioconda, Whistler's mother, that vicar
of Raeburn's gliding forever, perfectly balanced)

you tell me the tale of our shoulderblades,
how they're traces left over from seraphim wings
or their reticent buds, their seeds,
so either we've fallen, or feathery inklings
are waiting inside us to lift us and guide us.

Science has measured the sole distance
left for the mad, that span from moon to earth,
to the nearest inch.
They beamed lasers at mirrors placed on the surface.
How strangely unwavering light is.

On the train north, my feet huge
as tombstones on the opposite seat,
I'm much too percussive and lose
hours chewing over my Collected F. Scott:
For sale — baby shoes, never used.

Home and the moon's scattered over the lough.
I know why you're crying —
the dreamt-of mistake,
that slip of a thing folded into itself like
a badly injured or broken wing.

The Copier

imagining the tune

I take and tear the pages, bolt the lines,
mark in staves and crochets, quavers,
and make half a foot of unplayed music.

Stapled together, I raise it to hover
above like a halo, and slide it on. It sits
like a hat from a Christmas cracker

then slips to mask, the Lone Ranger's but wider,
more like Ned Kelly's helmet, and then lower
so the notes fit over my lips in a halfwit's

gap-toothed grin, before dropping again
to a white neck-brace for the man paralysed
now from the mouth on down.

trapped light

The radiance that moves across the plate glass
of the copier is nothing but the dawn horizon
strapped into a plastic box.

And those lightbulbs countersunk inside the ceiling,
well, they could be stars, up close, at a loss
for what to spend light on.

Not the VDU that hums its single tune,
is feverish and ill with sleeplessness,
and when night comes will save its screen
though the striplights burn themselves to filaments and out.

Only the cone that falls from the lamp squatting
abroad on my desk will ever share part of itself.

drafting

This last note will take an age to get right.
I came to this place by a circuitous route.

Writing it out will take me the rest of my time
and leave me angry and lost and ashamed.

It might be a list of the passed over and missing.
I file my docs and set up my out-of-office message.

The bulb pops when I enter the study.
Moonlight may just be sufficient to work by.

A Guide to Modern Warsaw

The striplights
that illuminate the working late

have made my block
a latticework of boxed-up stars and dark:

it looks like the negative and inverse
of a letter, black-lined by the censor,

attempting to explain through injured syntax
and discussion mainly on the weather

that what will come for us
is air-conditioned, plushly fast,

and moves so smoothly on its tracks
that we'll stay crumpled, dead to the world,

when it pauses near the skyscraper,
the first ever built in Warsaw,

which demonstrates its brand awareness
on the site of the Great Synagogue

with a massive Sony mark
countersigned at pavement level

by twenty-six graffiti tags, eleven
printed pamphlets advertising prostitutes

or lessons in the martial arts,
and nine pleas for missing dogs.

Notes towards a Final Definition: Work

It may well equate to weight
times the distance moved,
but bear in mind the gravity and angle.
I have been pushing a stone up a hill.

And it could be labeled weight alone.
Or that multiplied by solitude.
(If you shut your eyes those pores and lines
the paper has could well be skin.)

What troubles is a neat equation.
Nothing fits the algorithm for nicotine and coffee.
A secretary stood very close beside me in the lift.
I smelt latté mixed with fire on her breath.

The stenographer's gaze stalls in mid-air
as if she is playing from memory.

Auction (no reserve)

You have gotten away with murder.

Now where shall we begin?
A prime and tender man.

Own teeth. Own hair.

You could make another killing.

Do I hear a fiver?
Will someone give a quid?

I am holding for your offer.
I am stalling,
waiting,
willing.

Bid.

The Evening Forecast for the Region

The weatherman for Boston ponders whether, *I'd bet not*,
the snowstorm coming north will come to town tonight.

I swim around in bed. My head's attempting to begin
its routine shift down through the old transmission

to let me make the slope and slip the gearstick into neutral at the
    crown
before freewheeling down the ocean-road descent into the ghost town,

there, the coastal one, with a stone pier bare as skin, familiar
seafront houses hunched and boarded-over for the winter,

and beside the tattered nets a rowing boat lies upturned on the beach.
Aside from a mongrel, inside, asleep at someone's slippered feet,

everything faces the sea. But the plumbing's sighs are almost human.
Airlocks collect and slide from duct to duct so the radiators whine.

The hiding places grow further hidden. A priesthole's given over
to a spider's architecture. A well tries on a grassy manhole cover,

threaded, dangerous as fingers. An ivied sycamore in the forest at
    Drum Manor,
resonant and upright and empty as an organ pipe, where for a
    panicked hour

a boy will not be found. I arch one foot to scratch the other.
I would shed myself to segue into sleep. I would enter

but the opening is of a new off-Broadway *Hamlet*. The gulf is war.
This hiatus, my father's hernia. The cleft's a treble on the score

of Scott Joplin's 'Entertainer'. This respite is a care home,
the recess a playground. This division I slither into is a
    complicated sum:

thirteen over seven. I give in. I turn the television on.
The weatherman for Boston is discussing how, *Thank Heaven*,

the snowstorm missed, and turned, and headed out to sea.
Is it particularly human, this, to lie awake? To touch the papery

encircling bark but watch through a knot, and wait?
Everyone on earth is sleeping. I am the keel-scrape

beneath their tidal breathing which is shifting down through
    tempo
to the waveform of the sea. The gathered even draw and lift of air.

Further east a blizzard of homogenous decisions breathes above
the folding and unfolding pane and counterpane of waves

as if the white so loves the world it tries to make a map of it,
exact and blank to start again, but the sea will not stay under it.

The ricepaper wafers are melting. Millions of babynails cling
to the wind lifting hoarsely off the Atlantic. The whole thing

is mesmeric. For hours the snow will fall like rhythm.
                                                    Listen.

Appendix

The one we saw in the jar
had the pluperfect aura
of a worm hung in tequila,

though later, undercover, after
turning away from each other,
out of the blue, or wherever

it is that we wander in slumber,
suddenly you, or whoever *you* are
half-asleep, whisper

It was a reminder of other.

How could I not remember the summer
your vermicular organ turned fatter,
turned squatter, and left you the scar

that I brush with the tip of my finger,
a doubter, before sliding the duvet over
to cover that badge of danger and care?

The curtains surface in dawn's slow exposure.
Our neighbour starts up her car and you shiver.
Hushing our avenue's branches, the wind's timbre

is pitched closer to anger than wonder.

Notes

p. 21, "Remaindermen" — "fornenst" is a Northern Irish dialect word meaning facing, opposite.

p. 61, "The Last Saturday in Ulster" — "the last Saturday" is a phrase denoting the day (the last Saturday in August) that the Royal Black Preceptory (part of the Orange Order) have their main parade. The last Saturday traditionally marks the end of the parading calendar.

Nick Laird was born in 1975 in County Tyrone, Northern Ireland. He has lived in Warsaw and Boston, and now lives in London. His debut novel, *Utterly Monkey*, was published in America in January 2006 by Harper Perennial.

A KNOW-
NOTHING
BIRTHDAY

ad Book®

story by Michele Sobel Spirn
pictures by R. W. Alley

HarperCollinsPublishers

For Mom and Dad—Norma and Marvin Spirn—
and for Steve and Josh, as always
—M.S.S.

For Jared, whose birthday came
while the paint was still wet.
—R.W.A.

HarperCollins®, ✋®, and I Can Read Book®
are trademarks of HarperCollins Publishers Inc.

A Know-Nothing Birthday
Text copyright © 1997 by Michele Sobel Spirn
Illustrations copyright © 1997 by R. W. Alley
Printed in the U.S.A. All rights reserved.

Library of Congress Cataloging-in-Publication Data
Spirn, Michele.
  A Know-Nothing birthday / story by Michele Sobel Spirn ;
pictures by R. W. Alley
    p.   cm. — (An I can read book)
  Summary: Four foolish friends called the Know-Nothings have a birthday
celebration.
  ISBN 0-06-027273-2. — ISBN 0-06-027274-0 (lib. bdg.)
  [1. Birthdays—Fiction. 2. Friendship—Fiction. 3. Humorous stories.]
I. Alley, R. W. (Robert W.), ill. II. Title. III. Series.
PZ7.S7567K1   1997   96-18372
[E]—dc20   CIP
                                                             AC

2   3   4   5   6   7   8   9   10
❖

CONTENTS

WHOSE BIRTHDAY?

Boris, Morris, Doris, and Norris

were four good friends.

People called them Know-Nothings.

They didn't know much,

but they knew they liked each other.

Boris's birthday was coming.

He was afraid

his friends had forgotten.

He hummed "Happy Birthday."

"The bees hum so nicely,"

said Doris.

He sent himself birthday cards.

Norris said,

"Gosh, you have a lot of pen pals."

Boris put signs

all over the house.

"Thank you very much," Morris said,

"but it's not my birthday."

9

Boris tried again.

"I will bake a cake,"

he said to Norris.

Norris told Morris,

but Morris heard,

"Boris fell over a rake."

Morris ran to tell Doris.

"Boris fell over a rake!" he yelled.

Doris heard,

"Boris has an earache."

"We must help Boris," she said.

She got some pills.

Morris took some bandages.

13

Morris and Doris found

Boris and Norris eating cake.

"Boris, can you hear me?"

asked Doris.

"Of course," said Boris.

"Where's that nasty rake?"

asked Morris.

"What rake?" asked Boris.

"He seems to be all right.

He is eating cake,"

said Doris.

"That's what I told Morris,"

said Norris.

"No, you told me

that Boris had fallen over a rake,"

said Morris.

"And you told me

Boris had an earache," said Doris.

"Boris, are you all right?"

asked Norris.

"I am fine," said Boris.

"We are so happy

you are all right," said Doris.

And the Know-Nothings

gave Boris a big hug.

MANY HANDS

Doris looked at her calendar.

"Tomorrow is Boris's birthday!"

she cried.

"We must give him presents."

"What shall we get him?"

asked Morris.

"We will have to watch Boris
to find out what he wants,"
said Doris.

Morris watched Boris.

Boris was cleaning the windows.

"I could really use

another pair of hands

to help me,"

he said.

20

"Hands! He wants hands!"

cried Morris.

"What do you mean?"

asked Doris.

"The last time

I saw Boris

he had two hands."

"When I saw him

he had two hands,"

said Norris.

"He had two hands

when I saw him,"

said Morris.

Doris counted.

"That makes six hands.

That gives me an idea,"

she said.

Morris, Norris, and Doris

went to the biggest store in town.

They went in and out and in and out
and in and out and in and out
the revolving door.

"It is very hard

to get into this store," said Morris.

"May I help you?"

asked the saleswoman.

"We want to buy some gloves

for Boris," said Doris.

"Here are some nice ones,"

said the woman.

"We will take six," said Morris.

"One for each of his hands,"

said Doris.

"Boris sounds special,"

said the woman.

"Yes, he's very handy,"

said Morris, Norris, and Doris.

The Know-Nothings tried to leave.

This time they went out and in

and out and in and out and in

the revolving door.

Finally a big crowd pushed them out.

"That was a long ride,"

said Norris.

And Morris, Norris, and Doris
wobbled as they walked home
with their presents for Boris.

SURPRISE!

Doris heard someone

at the front door.

"Surprise!" she yelled.

"What surprise?" asked Norris.

"I am giving Boris

a surprise birthday party,"

said Doris.

"I am surprised," said Norris.

"But you are not Boris," said Doris.

"I love surprise parties,"

said Norris. "Can I help?"

"Sure," said Doris.

They heard someone at the door.

"Surprise!" yelled Doris and Norris.

"What surprise?" asked Morris.

"No surprise," said Doris.

"Why are you yelling *surprise*?"

asked Morris.

"We are giving Boris

a surprise birthday party,"

said Doris.

"Great!" said Morris.

"Can I surprise him too?"

"Okay," said Doris.

"But we have to find Boris

to surprise him."

They looked in the bathtub.

They looked under the beds.

They looked

up the chimney.

No Boris!

"Where can he be?" asked Morris.

"I don't know," said Doris.

"I have an idea," said Norris.

"Everyone knows

about food for thought.

We will have a snack

to help us think."

"You are so clever, Norris,"

said Morris.

"Hi," said Boris.

"Boris, what are you doing here?" asked Morris.

"I am having a birthday party," said Boris.

"But we are giving you a surprise birthday party," said Doris.

"I wish you had told me,"

said Boris.

"Now I am busy with my own party."

"What can we do?" asked Norris.

"We could have the surprise party
without Boris," said Morris.

"That would be a surprise!"

"I know," said Doris.

"Boris can have two parties.

Finish your party, Boris,

then we will surprise you."

"You are so clever, Doris,"

said Boris.

He lit the candles on his cake
and sang "Happy Birthday."
Then he blew them out.
"I am ready now," he said.

"Happy Birthday!"

yelled Morris, Doris, and Norris.

"What a surprise!" cried Boris.

"Open your presents," said Morris.

Boris opened the first box.

"Gloves! How nice!" he cried.

He opened the second box.

"Gloves again! Twice as nice!"

He opened the third box.

"Gloves! What a clever idea!"

"Thank you," Boris said.

"I thought you had forgotten
my birthday."

"How could we forget?" asked Doris.

"Aren't we your best friends?"

Then Doris, Morris, and Norris

helped Boris blow out

his birthday candles again.

They ate lots of cake.

And every now and then

his best friends yelled, "Surprise!"

so that Boris wouldn't forget

it was his birthday.